JOKE BOOK

6 YEAR OLD EDITION

TRY
NOT
TO
LAUGH
CHALLENGE™

Copyright© 2019 by Try Not to Laugh Challenge Joke Group

ALL RIGHTS RESERVED. By purchase of this book, you have been licensed one copy for personal use only. No part of this work may be reproduced, redistributed, or used in any form or by any means without prior written permission of the publisher and copyright owner.

Try Not To Laugh Challenge
BONUS PLAY

Join our Joke Club and get the Bonus Play PDF!

Simply send us an email to:

TNTLPublishing@gmail.com

and you will get the following:

- 10 Hilarious, Bonus Jokes
- An entry in our Monthly Giveaway of a $50 Amazon Gift card!

We draw a new winner each month and will contact you via email!

Good luck!

☺

WELCOME TO THE
TRY NOT TO LAUGH CHALLENGE!

RULES OF THE GAME:

★ Grab a friend or family member, a pen/pencil, and your comedic skills! Determine who will be "Jokester 1" and "Jokester 2".

★ Take turns reading the jokes aloud to each other, and check the box next to each joke you get a laugh from! Each laugh box is worth 1 point, and the pages are labeled to instruct and guide when it is each player's turn.

★ Once you have both completed telling jokes in the round, tally up your laugh points and mark it down on each score page! There is a total of 10 Rounds.

★ Play as many rounds as you like! Once you reach the last round, Round 10, tally up ALL points from the previous rounds to determine who is the CHAMPION LAUGH MASTER!

★ Round 11 - The Tie-Breaker Round.

In the event of a tie, proceed to Round 11. This round will be 'Winner Takes All!', so whoever scores more laugh points in this round alone, is crowned the CHAMPION LAUGH MASTER!

TIP: Use an expressive voice, facial expressions, and even silly body movement to really get the most out of each joke and keep the crowd laughing!

Now, it's time to play!

ROUND

1

 **JOKESTER 1**

Why was the man talking to a clock?

He was telling time!

⬜ LAUGH

What did the pencil call his friend?

Pen pal!

⬜ LAUGH

Did you hear about the door who got stuck?

He was in a jam!

☑ LAUGH

What do you call a baby dogfish?

A Puppy Guppy!

⬜ LAUGH

What did the feather say to the fan?

"You blow me away!"

☐ LAUGH

What's the alphabet's favorite drink?

T! (Tea)

☐ LAUGH

What did the cat say when he got hurt?

"Me-OUCH!"

☐ LAUGH

What does a dolphin say, when he's done eating?

"I'm FIN-ished!"

☐ LAUGH

Pass the book to Jokester 2! ➔

 **JOKESTER 2**

What do you call a competition of clowns?

A Goof-Off!

☐ LAUGH

How do you become a cowboy?

You get roped into it.

☐ LAUGH

Why did the elephant and the car get along?

They both have trunks!

☐ LAUGH

What's a ghost librarian's favorite thing to say?

"Boooooooooks!"

☐ LAUGH

 **JOKESTER 2**

What is a policeman's favorite office product?

The COP-y machine!

☐ LAUGH

Did you hear about the giant lizard, who climbed the building and shed his skin?

"Yeah, he SCALED the building!"

☐ LAUGH

What do you call a wild dog who can swim?

A Floaty Coyote!

☐ LAUGH

Why did the root beer wear sunglasses?

To hide from the POP-arazzi!

☐ LAUGH

Time to add up your points! →

13

SCORE BOARD

Add up each Jokester's laugh points
for this round!

JOKESTER 1

/8
Total

JOKESTER 2
/8
Total

ROUND WINNER

ROUND
2

What do you call it when someone makes a candy bar appear from thin air?

Magic Twix! (Tricks)

LAUGH

Why is baseball the richest sport?

It's the only sport with a diamond!

LAUGH

What do you call potato slices covered in cocoa?

Chocolate chips!

LAUGH

How do you catch an electric eel?

With a lightning rod!

LAUGH

 **JOKESTER 1**

What's Willy Wonka's favorite board game?

Candy Land!

○ LAUGH

Why are dalmatians bad at hide and seek?

They are easy to SPOT!

○ LAUGH

Where do cats keep their clothes?

The CLAWS-et!

○ LAUGH

What is a shoe's favorite sport?

SOCK-er!

○ LAUGH

Pass the book to Jokester 2! →

How do fishermen watch movies?

NET-flix!

LAUGH

How did the monkey find the bananas?

He kept his eyes PEELED!

LAUGH

Why did the worm move to a new hole?

He needed more wiggle room!

LAUGH

Where does a dog keep its car?

The BARK-ing lot!

LAUGH

What's the alphabet's favorite sport?

T-ball!

☐ LAUGH

What do you call it when lollipops box?

Sucker punching!

☐ LAUGH

What do you get when you put G.I. Joe on ice?

An Action Figure Skater!

☐ LAUGH

What's the best time to visit the forest?

TREE o'clock!

☐ LAUGH

Time to add up your points! →

19

SCORE BOARD

Add up each Jokester's laugh points for this round!

JOKESTER 1

/8

Total

JOKESTER 2

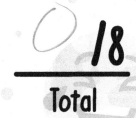

/8

Total

ROUND WINNER

ROUND
3

 **JOKESTER 1**

What is the ocean's weapon of choice?

Water gun!

LAUGH

Why do pirates love the Olympics?

Because of all the GOLD!

LAUGH

What is a stuffed animal's favorite fruit?

Teddy BEAR-ries! (Berries)

LAUGH

What's a duck's favorite baseball play?

LAUGH

A fowl ball!

What do you call playdough that acts goofy?

Silly Putty.

☐ LAUGH

What do you call it when a snake throws a tantrum?

A hisssssy fit!

☐ LAUGH

What's a kitchen table's favorite soda?

CHAIR-y Coke.

☐ LAUGH

What does a snowman eat for breakfast?

A bowl of Frosted Flakes.

☐ LAUGH

Pass the book to Jokester 2! →

Why couldn't anyone get into the piano's house?

She kept all her keys!

LAUGH

What's a wind-up toy's favorite game?

Twister!

LAUGH

What do you call a cold vegetable?

LAUGH

A CHILL-y pepper!

Why did the cat cross the road?

He felt like it!

LAUGH

What do scarecrows eat for breakfast?

STRAW-berries!

◻ LAUGH

What do rainbows use to write with?

Colored pencils!

◻ LAUGH

What dog loves technology?

Computer LABS!

◻ LAUGH

When do little bears wear uniforms?

When they go to Cub Scout meetings!

◻ LAUGH

Time to add up your points! ➝

SCORE BOARD

Add up each Jokester's laugh points for this round!

JOKESTER 1
$$\frac{\quad\quad\quad}{\text{Total}} \text{ /8}$$

JOKESTER 2
$$\frac{\quad\quad\quad}{\text{Total}} \text{ /8}$$

ROUND WINNER

ROUND

4

What's an art teacher's favorite nursery rhyme?

'Pop Goes The Easel!'

☐ LAUGH

What do foxes wear to keep their feet warm?

Fox socks!

☐ LAUGH

What animal communicates only through the telephone?

A croco-DIAL.

☐ LAUGH

What did the snake say to his Valentine?

"Can I have a kisssssss?"

☐ LAUGH

28

What did the duck say to the comedian?

"You QUACK me up!"

☐ LAUGH

What kind of parties do birthday candles like?

Big blowouts!

☐ LAUGH

What Disney movie do bears love most?

Peter PANDA!

☐ LAUGH

What do you call it when a small tree robs you?

A STICK-up!

☐ LAUGH

Pass the book to Jokester 2! ➜

What kind of dance can never be a ball?

A square dance!

☐ LAUGH

What do you get when you mix a raptor and a rhinoceros?

A Dino Rhino.

☐ LAUGH

Why couldn't the sun see the moon?

He forgot his sunglasses!

☐ LAUGH

The lollipop is always so nice to everyone! She's so SWEET.

☐ LAUGH

 **JOKESTER 2**

What did the vegetable farmer say when dinner was ready?

"Lettuce eat!" ☐ LAUGH

Where do houses go when they need new walls?

WAL-Mart, of course! ☐ LAUGH

What do you call a bunch of ducks stuck together?

DUCK-tape! ☐ LAUGH

What sound does the Easter frog make?

"Rabbit-Rabbit!" ☐ LAUGH

Time to add up your points! →

SCORE BOARD

Add up each Jokester's laugh points
for this round!

JOKESTER 1

$\dfrac{/8}{\text{Total}}$

JOKESTER 2

$\dfrac{/8}{\text{Total}}$

ROUND WINNER

ROUND
5

What did the bear give his friend on Valentine's Day?

A big, BEAR hug!

☐ LAUGH

Why was Dracula unable to give a speech?

Stage Bite. (Stage Fright)

☐ LAUGH

What did the cat say after his meal?

"That was PURRR-fect."

☐ LAUGH

What color is the flag of the United Ghosts of America?

Red, white, and BOO!

☐ LAUGH

What did the Sun answer, when the Moon asked where it was?

"I'm BRIGHT here!"

LAUGH

Why did the hand get a warm, fuzzy feeling?

He was falling in g-LOVE!

LAUGH

What do they call the winner of the Light Competition?

The Lamp Champ!

LAUGH

Why don't you throw walnuts on the ground?

Because then they'd be floor-nuts!

LAUGH

Pass the book to Jokester 2! ➞

What award show did Big Bird and Elmo like the most?

The OSCARS.

☐ LAUGH

Why was the car with a flat so restless?

It never got TIRE-D!

☐ LAUGH

What do you call a baby pig with a flying license?

A Piglet! (Pilot)

☐ LAUGH

Which letters make honey?

B's

☐ LAUGH

What did the rude cow say to the other cow on the bus?

"MOOO-ve over!"

LAUGH

What did baby Pepsi say to her dad?

"I love you, POP!"

LAUGH

What did the landing say to the steps?

"What are you STAIR-ing at?"

LAUGH

Why did the carriage driver get pulled over for speeding?

He couldn't hold his horses!

LAUGH

Time to add up your points! →

37

SCORE BOARD

Add up each Jokester's laugh points for this round!

 **JOKESTER 1**

$$\frac{\ \ /8\ \ }{\text{Total}}$$

 **JOKESTER 2**

$$\frac{\ \ /8\ \ }{\text{Total}}$$

_____
ROUND WINNER

ROUND

6

 **JOKESTER 1**

Did you hear about the clown who took six baths a day?

Yeah, he smelled funny.

LAUGH

How was the monster being rude at the dinner party?

He was GOBLIN everything up!

LAUGH

Which animal loves a cloudy day?

A RAIN-deer.

LAUGH

What is a dog's favorite kind of soap?

Sham-POODLE!

LAUGH

 **JOKESTER 1**

Why did mustard lose the race?

He couldn't KETCHUP! ☐ LAUGH

What do you call someone who's in charge of picking up sticks?

A Branch Manager! ☐ LAUGH

What kind of bean doesn't grow outside?

Jelly bean! ☐ LAUGH

Why did the cow have a garage sale?

She was MOOO-ving. ☐ LAUGH

Pass the book to Jokester 2! ➝

41

What color is a tantrum?

YELL-ow!

LAUGH

What is a frog's favorite fast food meal?

A Hoppy Meal with flies.

LAUGH

What clothes should you always wear to school?

Smarty pants!

LAUGH

What is the coolest superhero haircut?

The mo-HULK! (Mohawk)

LAUGH

JOKESTER 2

What's a cat's favorite game?

Mouse Trap!

☐ LAUGH

What is the nose's favorite sport?

☐ LAUGH

Running!

Where does a car eat its food?

On a license PLATE!

☐ LAUGH

What's a magician's favorite cereal?

Trix!

☐ LAUGH

Time to add up your points! →

SCORE BOARD

Add up each Jokester's laugh points for this round!

JOKESTER 1

$\dfrac{\text{/8}}{\text{Total}}$

JOKESTER 2

$\dfrac{\text{/8}}{\text{Total}}$

_____

ROUND WINNER

ROUND

7

What's a carpet's favorite sport?

RUG-by!

☐ LAUGH

What sport are Santa's elves good at?

BOX-ing!

☐ LAUGH

What's a snake's favorite board game?

Rattleship!

☐ LAUGH

Why was the mother insect sad?

She had her FLEA-lings hurt!

☐ LAUGH

What is a bug doctor's favorite superhero?

Spiderman!

LAUGH ☐

What do robots win in the Olympics?

Metals!

LAUGH ☐

What do you call it when a washer meets an oven?

Shake and bake!

LAUGH ☐

What do you call a test on soda?

A POP quiz!

LAUGH ☐

Pass the book to Jokester 2! →

What do you call a drawing of soup?

Oodles O' Doodles.

LAUGH

What is the laziest vegetable out there?

Couch potato!

LAUGH

What did the fish say to his girlfriend?

"You're a great CATCH!"

LAUGH

Why did the ghost feel so lonely?

There was no-BODY around him.

LAUGH

 **JOKESTER 2**

What's a dog's best sport?

Chase-ball!

☐ LAUGH

Why did the strawberry ask for help?

He was in a jam!

☐ LAUGH

What superhero did the tomato want to be when he grew up?

SOUP-erman!

☐ LAUGH

What bug likes clocks?

Ticks!

☐ LAUGH

Time to add up your points! →

SCORE BOARD

Add up each Jokester's laugh points for this round!

JOKESTER 1

$$\frac{}{\text{Total}} \, /8$$

JOKESTER 2

$$\frac{}{\text{Total}} \, /8$$

ROUND WINNER

ROUND

8

 **JOKESTER 1**

What do you call a flower who likes to spin around?

Dizzy Daisy.

LAUGH

What did the skeptical artist say, when someone told him to mix red and white?

"I don't PINK so!"

LAUGH

What do you call it when your foot steps in jelly?

Toe JAM.

LAUGH

What do you call an annoyed vegetable?

Grum-PEA.

LAUGH

What do celebrities eat on hot summer days?

POP-sicles.

LAUGH

What vegetable is always dizzy?

SPIN-ach.

LAUGH

What is a turtle's favorite food?

Hard shell tacos.

LAUGH

What do puppies say when they see each other?

"What's up, dog?"

LAUGH

Pass the book to Jokester 2! ➔

# JOKESTER 2

What do you call a spider in a snowstorm?

A BRRRRR-antula!

LAUGH

How does a mule open the barn door?

With a don-KEY.

LAUGH

What do you call a sleeping cow?

A Bull-dozer.

LAUGH

What insect would enjoy medicine?

A cater-PILL-ar!

LAUGH

What do you call a slow seamstress?

A Cloth Sloth!

LAUGH

What do balding boars wear?

Pig wigs!

LAUGH

What do you call a yellow, checkered crustacean from New York City?

A Taxi Cab Crab!

LAUGH

What do you do if you see a monster under a bridge?

Stop, drop, and TROLL!

LAUGH

Time to add up your points! →

SCORE BOARD

Add up each Jokester's laugh points for this round!

JOKESTER 1

/8
___
Total

JOKESTER 2

/8
___
Total

ROUND WINNER

ROUND

9

 **JOKESTER 1**

What animal can't see color?

Zebra!

LAUGH

Why don't eggs ride roller coasters?

They'll get scrambled!

LAUGH

Why would a game of musical chairs go to a barber?

To get a CHAIR-cut!

LAUGH

What do you call clothes that you wear in a sauna?

SWEAT-ers.

LAUGH

 **JOKESTER 1**

What's the funniest room in a school?

The LAUGH-ateria!

☐ LAUGH

What do you call a dog toy in the dishwasher?

Squeaky clean!

☐ LAUGH

Why is the door so shy?

He won't open up!

☐ LAUGH

What is the river's favorite dessert?

Ice STREAM!

☐ LAUGH

Pass the book to Jokester 2! →

 **JOKESTER 2**

Why couldn't the frog skip town?

Someone TOAD his car!

◻ LAUGH

What fish doesn't like getting wet?

A CAT-fish!

◻ LAUGH

Why can't rattlesnakes be trusted to keep a secret?

They have a rattle tail! (Tattle tail)

◻ LAUGH

Why was the elephant banned from the YMCA?

He wore his trunks on his head.

◻ LAUGH

 **JOKESTER 2**

Who is the most famous in the ocean?

The STAR-fish!

☐ LAUGH

How did the mustang win the big race?

☐ LAUGH

He was wearing his Nike HORSE-shoes!

What did the squirrel say about the big news?

"It was NUTS!"

☐ LAUGH

What vehicle did the camel drive to pick up the garbage?

A HUMP-truck.

☐ LAUGH

Time to add up your points! ➔

SCORE BOARD

Add up each Jokester's laugh points for this round!

JOKESTER 1  /18
_____
Total

JOKESTER 2 /18
_____
Total

_____

ROUND WINNER

ROUND
10

 **JOKESTER 1**

Why does the dog keep getting in trouble?

Too much RUFF housing!

☐ LAUGH

What do fish need to make a fish fire?

Fish sticks.

☐ LAUGH

What do sea turtle's put on their toast?

JELLY-fish.

☐ LAUGH

What do mashed potatoes open doors with?

A Tur-KEY!

☐ LAUGH

 **JOKESTER 1**

What's Spiderman's favorite hobby?

Surfing the WEB!

☐ LAUGH

Why was the library so tall?

It had a lot of STORIES!

☐ LAUGH

What vehicle does a genius use?

Smart car.

☐ LAUGH

What do you call it when your floor is on fire?

Rug burn!

☐ LAUGH

Pass the book to Jokester 2! ➜

 **JOKESTER 2**

What did the drummer use when he got scraped?

A BAND-Aid.

☐ LAUGH

What do you call a floor mat with pixie dust on it?

A magic carpet!

☐ LAUGH

What does Anna's rock band wear?

Band-ANNA's!

☐ LAUGH

What do you call a potato wearing socks?

Hot pota-TOES!

☐ LAUGH

 **JOKESTER 2**

What happens when a banana drives too fast?

It peels out! ☐ LAUGH

What did one frog say to another?

"TOAD you so!" ☐ LAUGH

What did the mom bee tell her children while scolding them?

"You better BEE-have!" ☐ LAUGH

Why was the jelly late to work?

There was a traffic JAM. ☐ LAUGH

Time to add up your points! →

SCORE BOARD

Add up each Jokester's laugh points for this round!

JOKESTER 1

/8
――――――
Total

JOKESTER 2

/8
――――――
Total

――――――――――――――

ROUND WINNER

Add up all your points from each round.
The Jokester with the most points is crowned

The Laugh Master!

In the event of a tie, continue to Round 11
- The Tie-Breaker Round!

JOKESTER 1

Grand Total

JOKESTER 2

Grand Total

THE LAUGH MASTER

ROUND
11
TIE-BREAKER
(Winner Takes ALL!)

 **JOKESTER 1**

What's the chilliest reptile?

A bl-lizard!

◻ LAUGH

What is a cat's favorite color?

PURRR-ple.

◻ LAUGH

What kind of animal always knows what time it is?

A Watchdog.

◻ LAUGH

What's a pig's favorite tool?

A HAM-mer.

 ◻ LAUGH

 **JOKESTER 1**

The lion is always trying to be like everyone else. He's such a copy CAT!

○ LAUGH

Why was the dog a bad pilot?

His landings were always RUFF.

○ LAUGH

Why couldn't the potato get on the rollercoaster?

He's just small fry.

○ LAUGH

What do you call a dog who leaves stains?

Spot!

○ LAUGH

Pass the book to Jokester 2! →

What insect is best on toast?

A BUTTER-fly.

◯ LAUGH

What kind of reptile can keep a beat?

A SNAP-ping Turtle.

◯ LAUGH

What did the bossy phone say when it got plugged in?

"I'm in CHARGE!"

◯ LAUGH

What is Donkey Kong's favorite fighting style?

KONG-FU!

◯ LAUGH

How do dogs use the phone?

With their COLLAR!

○ LAUGH

What do dolphins say when they go underwater?

"You can't SEA me."

○ LAUGH

How does a cat make his food?

It starts from SCRATCH.

○ LAUGH

What do you call a comb made of rabbits?

A HARE brush.

○ LAUGH

Time to add up your points! →

Add up all your points from the
Tie-Breaker Round.
The Jokester with the most points is crowned

The Laugh Master!

JOKESTER 1 /8
Total

JOKESTER 2 /8
Total

THE LAUGH MASTER

Check out our

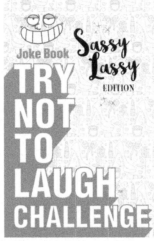

Visit our Amazon Store at:

other joke books!

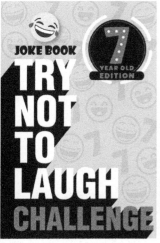

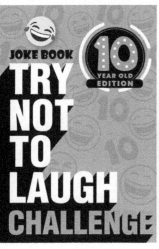
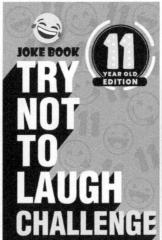
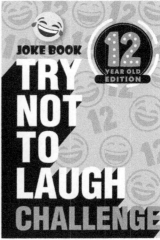

www.Amazon.com/author/CrazyCorey

Made in the USA
Monee, IL
06 February 2021

59787361R00046